AMAZING
MAGIC TRICKS

Filled with fantastic tricks to astound your friends!

ILLUSTRATED BY
DAVID MOSTYN

Dover Publications, Inc.
Mineola, New York

THIS BOOK IS DEDICATED TO THE FOLLOWING PEOPLE

My Uncle Matt, who showed the rest of the family just how much fun magic could be whenever we gathered. He could keep a roomful of people spellbound – and then fill the same room with helpless laughter.

Tommy Cooper, the comic whose magical "mistakes" brought tears to my eyes. His ability to get things wrong – when in fact he was an accomplished magician – also showed the importance of laughter.

But most of all my children – Jamie, Anna and Thomas – for their patient tolerance of a wacky father.

This Dover edition, first published in 2014,
is an unabridged republication of the work originally
published in 2013 by Arcturus Publishing Limited, London.

ISBN-13: 978-0-486-78034-4
ISBN-10: 0-486-78034-1

78034101   2014
www.doverpublications.com

Written by Thomas Canavan
Illustrated by David Mostyn
Designed by Emma Randall
Edited by Patience Coster

CONTENTS

A MESSAGE FROM THE MAGICIAN

You are about to enter a world of disappearances and reappearances, of numbers changing and numbers guessed out of thin air, of laughter, sleight of hand and mind games. It's a world where what you see isn't always what you get – it might be something very different, and unexpected. This is the world of magic.

This book contains dozens of tricks for you to perform – in front of an audience of one or a crowd of one hundred. You will learn the best ways to prepare for each trick, how to involve the audience and sometimes even what to wear to give the trick that extra bit of excitement and mystery.

Performing magic is a bit like tickling – it's almost impossible to do to yourself! But if you do it to someone else, that person feels helpless as he or she curls up with laughter. This is part of the secret. The tickler (the magician) is the one in control. The other person is the willing victim.

Although magic is about control, it's really about fun, and about bringing people together. Your audience knows you're not out to hurt them or make them feel bad. They really want you to succeed; and knowing this should give you confidence.

The tips in this book will help you to understand that practice really does make perfect. And remember – once you have become a magician, you must never give away the secrets of your tricks!

THE MAGICIAN'S PLEDGE

I promise not to reveal the secrets of magic to those who are not magicians.

I promise to rehearse these magic tricks over and over again before attempting to perform them in front of an audience.

I promise to respect my art, the art of magic.

Magician's Signature

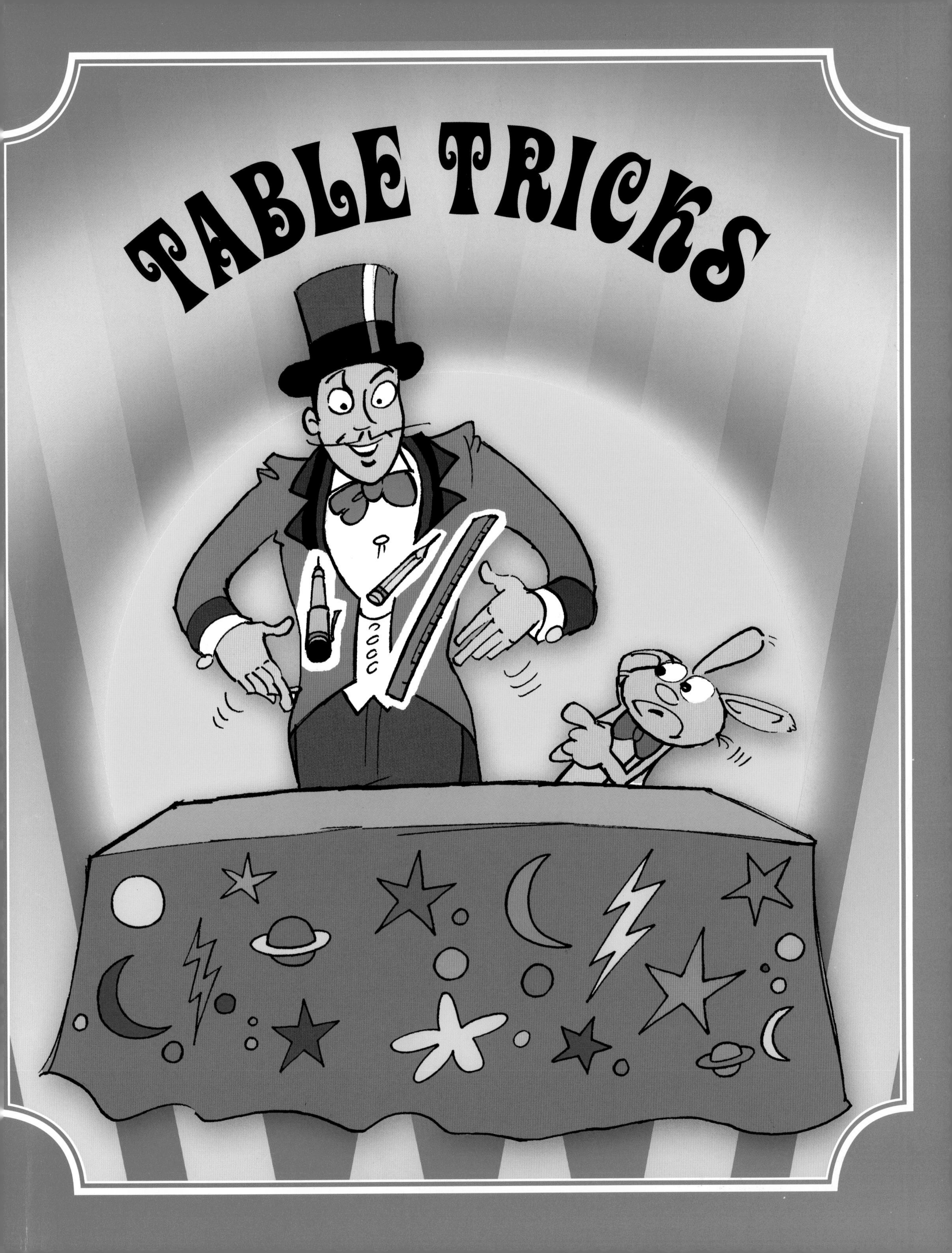
TABLE TRICKS

THE RISING PEN

ILLUSION

The magician casts a spell over a ballpoint pen. At his command, the pen rises through his clenched fist.

1 Prior to the trick, the magician finds a small, thin elastic band and a pen with a tight, hooked clip. He loops the elastic band around his right index finger.

2 To perform the trick, the magician holds up the pen with his left hand and tells the audience he is going to cast a spell over it. He hands it round so that they can see it is not a trick pen.

3 The magician stares hard at the pen and says: "Prepare to move." He slowly puts his right hand around his left, making sure to keep the elastic band hidden from the audience.

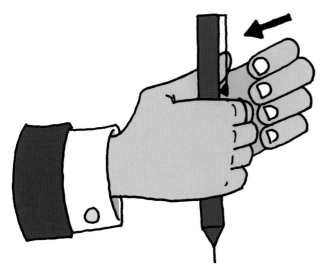

4 He slides the pen, writing point down, into his clenched right hand so that the clip catches the elastic band. Then he distracts the audience with some hand rolling.

5 During this rolling, he lets the pen flip over so that the writing point faces up. The pen is still in his cupped right hand, looped onto the elastic band.

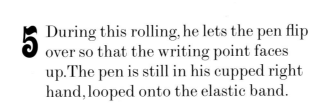

6 The magician continues muttering spells and moving his hands while secretly pulling the pen down so that the elastic stretches.

THE RISING PEN

7 He stops moving his hands and says the spell is cast. He holds the pen tight with his right hand and removes his left hand with a flourish.

8 The magician now commands the pen to rise slowly. He allows it to do this by releasing his grip gradually. The elastic band will slacken. If he releases his grip more quickly, the pen will spring up in his hand.

MAGIC TIP!
USE A PEN WITH A TIGHT CLIP.

WHICH TOY DID YOU CHOOSE?

ILLUSION

When an audience member secretly points to one of three toys on a table, the magician is mysteriously able to identify it.

1 This trick depends on two things – a good number of spectators and a partner who's in on the trick.

2 Before doing the trick, the magician and partner agree that the toy on the magician's right will be number 1, the middle toy will be number 2, and the toy on the magician's left will be number 3.

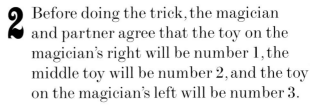

WHICH TOY DID YOU CHOOSE?

3 The magician turns his back to the toys and asks a volunteer to point at one of them. The other spectators note which toy has been chosen (one of those spectators is the magician's secret partner).

4 The magician turns round again and concentrates on the three toys. He moves closer, smells them and listens to them – to make it look as though he's picking up secret information.

5 He looks into the distance while he concentrates even harder. He makes sure he can see his partner, who blinks (or winks) once, twice, or three times to signal which toy was chosen (number 1, 2 or 3).

6 The magician looks once more at the toys, then points to the one that was indicated by his partner.

COUNTING CONFUSION

1 The magician places three coins of the same value on the table. He says he will use them to keep track of his counting.

ONE...

2 He picks them up one by one, counting "one," "two," and "three."

SIX

3 Then he puts them out again, counting "four," "five," and "six."

4 Saying "seven," the magician picks up one coin. Then he touches the other two, calling them "eight" and "nine."

5 He places the coin from his hand back on the table, calling it "ten."

COUNTING CONFUSION

6 The magician gathers up the coins and hands them to a spectator. He asks the spectator to repeat this simple counting.

7 The spectator begins by counting as she puts the coins down, not as she picks them up. This means she can never get the trick to work!

PEPPER CHASE

ILLUSION

A volunteer is invited to stick his finger into a bowl of water with pepper floating on the surface. Nothing happens. When the water is calm again, the magician does the same thing and the pepper scoots away from his finger.

1 Prior to the trick, the magician squeezes some washing-up liquid onto his index finger.

2 To perform the trick, the magician pours water into a shallow soup bowl until it is nearly full.

PEPPER CHASE

3 He sprinkles or grinds pepper over the water until the surface is almost covered.

4 The magician then asks a volunteer to dip his finger into the water. Nothing much happens.

5 The magician waits for the water to become calm again. Then he dips his index finger into the water.

6 The pepper zooms away from his finger to the edge of the bowl.

MAGIC ICE HOIST

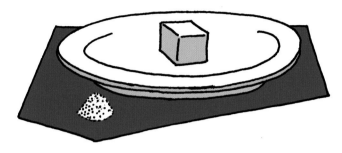

ILLUSION

The magician lays a piece of string on top of an ice cube and concentrates for a while. Then he takes each end of the string and lifts. The ice cube sticks to the string.

1 The magician puts an ice cube in the middle of a dinner plate. Beneath the lip of the plate – out of view of the audience – he places a small pile of table salt about the size of a grape.

MAGIC TIP!
TO DISTRACT THE AUDIENCE, SPEND TIME LEARNING HOW TO SPRINKLE SALT WITH ONE HAND WHILE WAVING YOUR OTHER HAND ABOUT!

2 The magician holds up a piece of string about the length of his lower arm. He says he will lift the ice cube off the plate with the string, without tying knots or making loops.

3 He hands the string round for the spectators to check. Then he lays it across the top of the ice cube.

4 The magician says some magic words and waves his arms around. Still waving with one hand, he lowers the other and takes a large pinch of salt from under the plate.

MAGIC ICE HOIST

5 He crosses and uncrosses his hands over the plate. On one of these crossings, he lets the salt feed out from between his fingers onto the top of the string.

6 The magician continues to move his hands, blocking the view of the ice cube as the salt dissolves. He mutters some special made-up magic words as he does this.

OOBA, KOOBA, ZINGLE, ZOO

7 After about 15 seconds, the magician takes hold of each end of the string. He pulls so that the string is taut, then lifts slowly. The ice cube remains attached to the string as he does so.

STICKING PENCILS

ILLUSION

The magician casts a spell while a volunteer holds two pencils together. When the volunteer tries to pull the pencils apart, he finds they are stuck together magically!

1 The magician takes two new (unsharpened) wooden pencils with completely flat ends. He holds the pencils up and hands them round for the audience to check.

2 He asks for a strong volunteer to come up and hold a pencil in each hand.

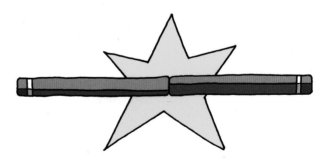

3 The magician gets the volunteer to hold the pencils together so that the ends are touching.

STICKING PENCILS

60...59...58...

...4...3...2...1

4 The magician asks the volunteer to press the pencils together as hard as he can for one minute. The magician gets the spectators to count down from 60 until the minute is up.

5 As the spectators count, the magician waves his hands slowly over the pencils.

6 When the minute is up, the magician says that he has magically locked the pencils together. He asks the volunteer to pull them apart, but it can't be done!

MAGIC FACT
THE VOLUNTEER'S MUSCLES "LOCK" AND KEEP PUSHING THE PENCILS TOGETHER, EVEN WHEN THE VOLUNTEER STOPS TRYING TO PUSH.

JUMPING COIN

1 The magician shows the audience two identical small coins.

2 He places a coin in each of his hands. The first coin should sit in the middle of his left hand. The second should sit on the bulge below his right thumb.

3 The magician flips his hands over quickly, which makes the coin in the right hand jump over to the left as he slams them down on the table.

JUMPING COIN

4 He says he has made one of the coins magically jump to his other hand. Slowly he turns his right hand over. There is no coin underneath!

NOT THERE!

5 Now he lifts his left hand. Both coins are there!

MAGIC FACT
THE COIN IN THE MAGICIAN'S RIGHT HAND REALLY DOES "JUMP" ACROSS TO HIS LEFT HAND.

KETCHUP CATCH-UP

ILLUSION

The magician uses his powers to levitate a sachet of ketchup inside a bottle of water.

1 Prior to the trick, the magician collects several ketchup sachets. He tests them one by one by dropping them into a bowl of water. He chooses a sachet that floats, but doesn't rise right to the top.

2 Next he removes the labels from a large, empty plastic cola bottle.

KETCHUP CATCH-UP

3 The magician begins the trick by showing the sachet of ketchup to the audience. Then he places it inside the plastic bottle.

4 The magician fills the bottle with water and screws on the cap.

5 He holds up the bottle so the spectators can see the ketchup packet floating halfway down.

ONE, TWO, THREE

6 Now he says he will command the ketchup to sink. He waves his hand in time with his count – "one," "two," "THREE." On the third count, he gives the bottle a slight squeeze. The ketchup sinks.

7 He counts again, but this time on the third count he stops squeezing. The ketchup rises again.

BALLS OF FUN

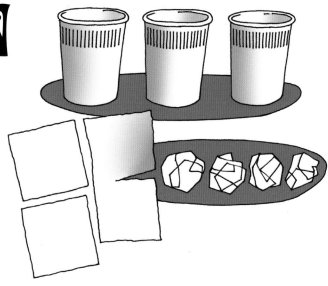

ILLUSION

The magician gets paper balls to pass through a plastic cup.

1 Prior to the trick, the magician finds three identical large plastic cups. He tears a paper napkin into four equal pieces and scrunches them into balls.

2 The magician puts one of the paper balls into one of the cups. He stands this cup on the table so that the spectators can't see inside it.

3 To perform the trick, the magician tells the spectators they will see some real magic with the simplest things – three paper balls and three plastic cups. He lines the cups up and puts a paper ball on the spectators' side of each one. The secret fourth ball is out of sight in the middle cup.

4 Now the magician flips the cups over. He flips the middle cup over quickly so that the ball doesn't fall out.

5 He puts a paper ball on the upturned middle cup and stacks the other two cups on top.

6 The magician says: "Now for some magic!" He taps the cups lightly with his wand. Then he lifts up the stack to show that the ball has gone all the way through!

7 The magician turns the cups the right way up and then dismantles the stack. The ball he placed on the upturned cup is now at the bottom of the middle cup.

8 The magician flips this cup over to cover the first ball (the one that "went through" the stack), and lines up the other cups on either side. (Now there are two balls under the middle cup, but the audience thinks there is only one.)

29

BALLS OF FUN

9 The magician places a paper ball on the middle cup and stacks the two empty cups over it.

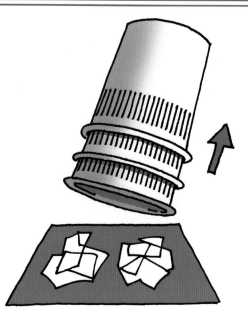

MAGIC TIP!
THIS TRICK DEPENDS ON YOUR ABILITY TO FLIP THE CUP OVER BEFORE THE BALL FALLS OUT. MAKE SURE YOU REHEARSE THIS BEFORE PERFORMING THE TRICK.

10 He taps the cups lightly twice and lifts the stack. There are now two balls underneath!

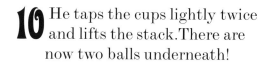

11 The magician pulls the stack apart and lines up the cups for the last time. He makes sure to cover the two paper balls with the cup that contains the hidden ball. With three balls now under the middle cup (the spectators think there are two), the magician puts the last ball on the middle cup and stacks the others on top.

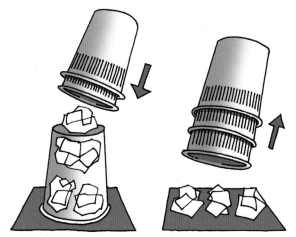

12 He taps the cups three times, lifts up the stack and – surprise! – all three balls are underneath!

SHOCKING STRAW

1 The magician sits behind a table and sets a drinking straw in front of him. It should be laid about half an arm's length away.

2 The magician says he will use the magnetic force of static electricity to push the straw away from him.

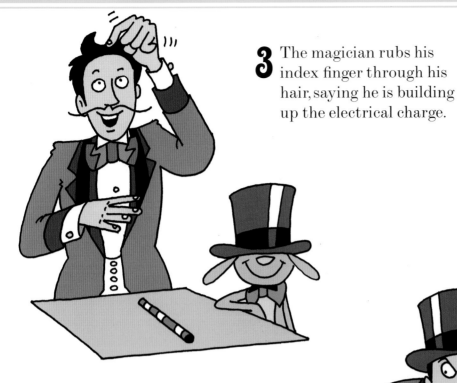

3 The magician rubs his index finger through his hair, saying he is building up the electrical charge.

4 He holds this finger over the middle of the straw, without touching it. He moves his finger forward slowly. As he does so, he secretly blows on his side of the straw. The magician takes care not to change the expression on his face as he blows. He stops moving his finger and blowing at the same time.

5 Finally he calls for volunteers from the audience to try the trick. They fail!

BOUNCING APPLE

1 A table and chair are needed for this trick. A low table or even a desk works, as long as the spectators can't see the magician's feet.

ILLUSION

The magician bounces an apple off the floor as if it were a rubber ball.

2 The trick begins with the magician sitting behind the table with an apple in front of him.

3 He picks up the apple and acts as if he's about to take a bite from it. He stops, sniffs it and says: "Maybe this one isn't ripe. I'd better test it."

4 He holds the apple at shoulder height …

5 …then he brings it down quickly, so that it goes out of the spectators' sight behind the table.

6 While doing this, the magician does two more things at the same time: he taps his foot on the ground and flips his wrist so that the apple flicks up in the air.

BOUNCING APPLE

7 It sounds – and looks – as though the apple has bounced off the floor and back into the air.

8 The magician catches the apple. He says: "Good bounce – it must be ripe!" and takes a bite from it.

UNFOLDABLE TOWEL

ILLUSION

The magician tries to fold an ordinary hand towel but it keeps bulging in unlikely directions.

1 Prior to the trick, the magician gets some practice holding a table fork with the handle pinched between his thumb and index finger.

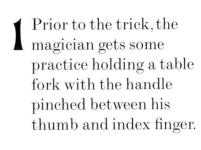

2 To perform the trick, the magician reaches into a box containing "an ordinary hand towel." But a fork is hidden in the towel.

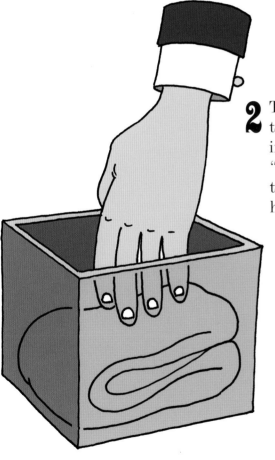

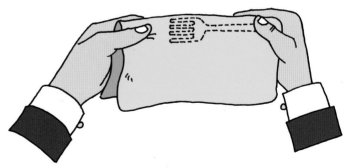

3 The magician picks up the towel, continuing to hide the fork by folding the towel over it and holding one end of the fold in his right hand. He holds the other end of the fold in his left hand. (This takes practice!)

UNFOLDABLE TOWEL

4 The magician shows the towel to the audience, still holding it tight with both hands. The fork can't be seen under the fold. The magician shows the audience the front and back of the towel, like a bullfighter twirling his cape.

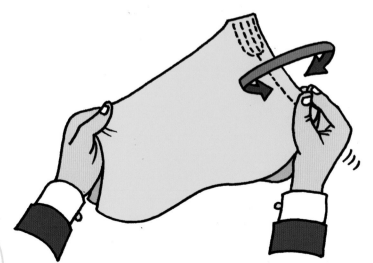

5 He tries to fold the towel, twisting his right wrist slightly so that the fork pokes into the fold and makes the towel rise up.

6 The magician looks surprised, and lets the fork go back down again. He continues raising and lowering the towel, staring at it as though he can't believe his eyes.

7 The magician finishes the trick by seeming to scrunch up the towel, but he's really scrunching it around the fork.

8 He puts the scrunched-up towel (with the fork hidden inside) back in the box.

THE STICKY SPOON

ILLUSION

A spoon seems to be stuck magically to the palm of the magician's hand.

1 For this trick, the magician needs to wear a long-sleeved shirt that will cover a wristwatch.

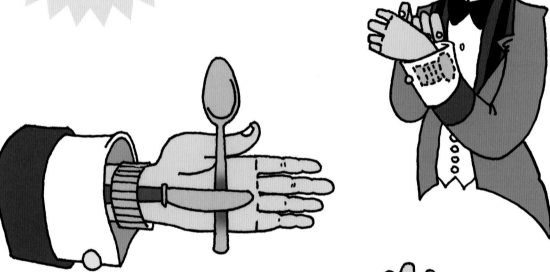

2 Prior to the trick, he slides a butter-knife under his watch-strap so that the blade is snug against the palm of his left hand. Next he slides the handle of a spoon under the blade of the knife. The ends of the spoon should jut out above and below the magician's palm.

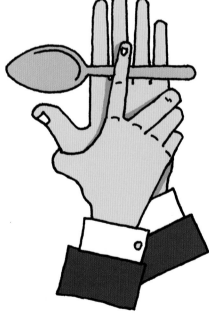

3 To begin the trick, the magician grabs his left wrist with his right hand so that his fingers are pointing in the same direction. He stretches out his right index finger to cover the knife blade.

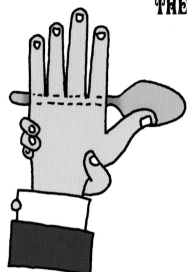

4 The magician holds up his hands so that the spectators see the spoon "stuck" behind his left hand.

5 Still holding his hands together, he turns them to show the other side. The audience can see that his right finger was holding the spoon in place. So he says: "OK – you saw through that one – I'll have to try something else!"

6 Keeping his hands together, the magician turns them back to their original position. Then he removes his right hand and waves it. The spoon is still stuck to his left hand!

41

BOUNCING HANKIE

ILLUSION

The magician pulls out a handkerchief to mop his brow. He throws it to the ground, but it bounces back up again!

1 Prior to the trick, the magician finds a very bouncy ball (about the size of a golf ball).

2 He wraps the ball in a thin handkerchief and stuffs it into his pocket.

3 On completing the previous trick, the magician says, "Phew – that was tiring! I need to mop my brow." He pulls the handkerchief out of his pocket. Without opening it, he uses it to mop his brow.

4 Then he throws the handkerchief straight down onto the hard floor, as if he's getting rid of it.

5 The handkerchief bounces back up, and the magician catches it and puts it back in his pocket.

6 Keeping a straight face, he says, "Now – where was I?" and moves on to the next trick.

MAGIC TIP!
MAGICIANS CALL QUICK TRICKS "THROWAWAY GAGS." THIS EASY TRICK IS A THROWAWAY GAG THAT ALWAYS GETS A LAUGH!

THE WRONG CARD

ILLUSION

The spectator picks a card, then the deck is placed in a bag. The magician keeps selecting the wrong card and gets so frustrated that he stamps on the bag. When he pulls his foot out, the chosen card is stuck to the bottom of his shoe!

1 Prior to the trick, the magician chooses a card and places it in the deck second from the top. He tapes a duplicate card to the bottom of his shoe, face side up.

2 To perform the trick, the magician places the cards face down and splits the deck in half, placing the halves side by side.

3 He takes the first card from the top half of the deck and places it on the bottom half. He now asks a spectator to pick the next card in the pile (the prepared card). The spectator looks at it, remembers it and shuffles it back into the deck.

THE WRONG CARD

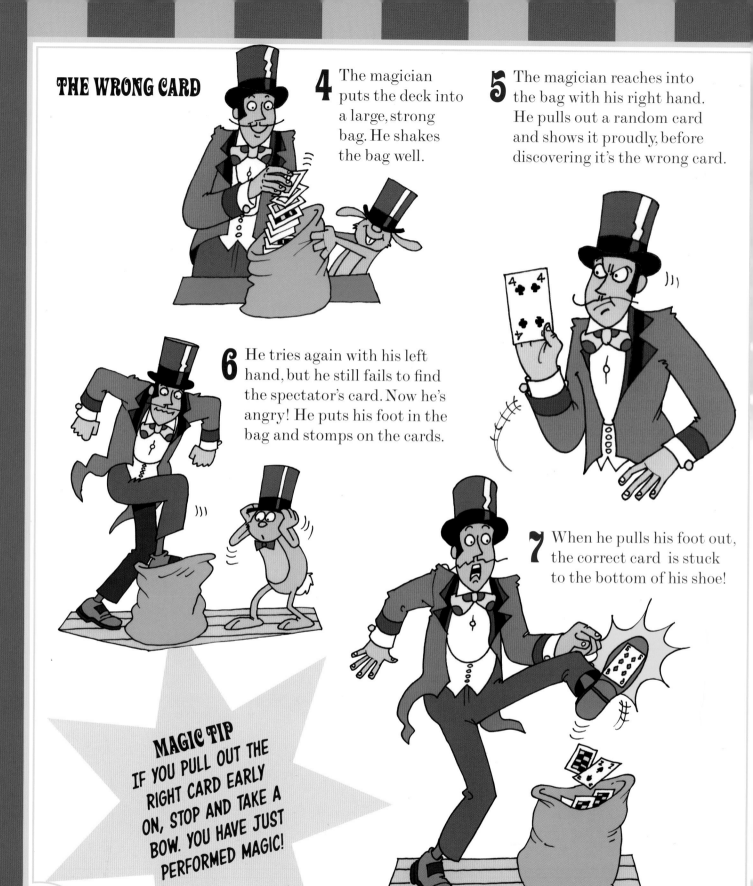

4 The magician puts the deck into a large, strong bag. He shakes the bag well.

5 The magician reaches into the bag with his right hand. He pulls out a random card and shows it proudly, before discovering it's the wrong card.

6 He tries again with his left hand, but he still fails to find the spectator's card. Now he's angry! He puts his foot in the bag and stomps on the cards.

7 When he pulls his foot out, the correct card is stuck to the bottom of his shoe!

MAGIC TIP
IF YOU PULL OUT THE RIGHT CARD EARLY ON, STOP AND TAKE A BOW. YOU HAVE JUST PERFORMED MAGIC!

THIMBLE ON THE GO

ILLUSION

A thimble seems miraculously to jump from one of the magician's fingers to another.

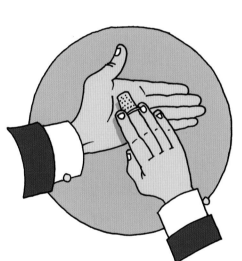

1 The magician slips a thimble onto the middle finger of his right hand. He makes sure the spectators see him do this.

2 He rests the index and middle fingers of his right hand against the palm of his left hand. Again, he makes sure the spectators see this.

3 The magician says that he will make the thimble jump from one finger to another on the count of three.

THIMBLE ON THE GO

4 He taps his index and middle fingers against his left palm three times, counting "one," "two," "three." Between taps he raises his right hand about one hand's length above his left.

ONE...TWO...
THREE!

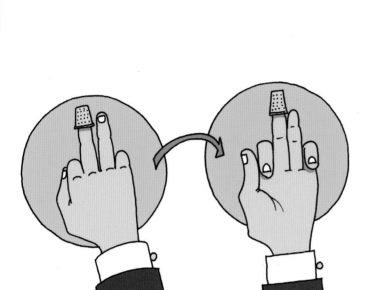

5 On the third tap, as he lowers his right hand, he curls his index finger under and extends his third finger.

6 This makes it look as though the thimble has jumped fingers.

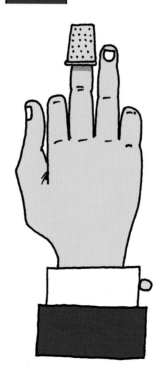

CRAZY CANDLE

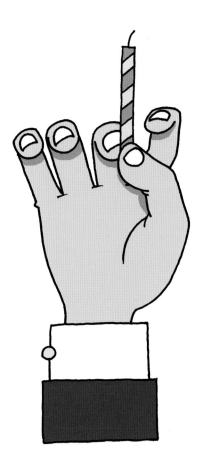

ILLUSION

The magician tells the spectators he can light a candle just by concentrating on it. He holds it tight up against his forehead, opens his hand – and there's a big surprise!

1 The magician holds up a small birthday candle in his right hand. He pinches it slightly with his thumb and middle finger. His palm should be facing away from the spectators.

2 He tells the spectators that he can light the candle just by concentrating on it. The magician looks hard at the candle for a few seconds. Nothing happens. "Hmm . . ." he says. "I need to concentrate a little harder – I'll put the candle closer to my brain." He continues to hold the candle in the same way.

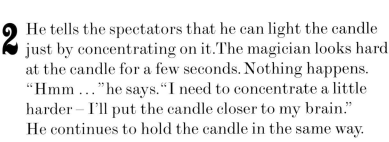

CRAZY CANDLE

3 "Right – now!" he says and, in a motion to move the candle closer to his head, he passes his left hand in front of the candle. As he does this, the magician loosens his grip. The candle falls into his right palm and he closes his hand over it. At the same time he closes his left hand (so it appears that the left hand is now clasped around the candle.)

4 The motion with the left hand finishes at the magician's forehead. He says, "Now I can really concentrate." He looks at the spectators and says: "Help me to concentrate hard on this candle and we can get it to light." As the spectators look up at the magician's left hand, he lowers his right hand and secretly drops the candle.

5 The magician says: "On the count of three, I'll open my hand and the candle will be lit. One … two … THREE!" He opens his hand, but there's nothing there! The magician says: "Whoops! Wrong trick!"

MAGICAL ESCAPES

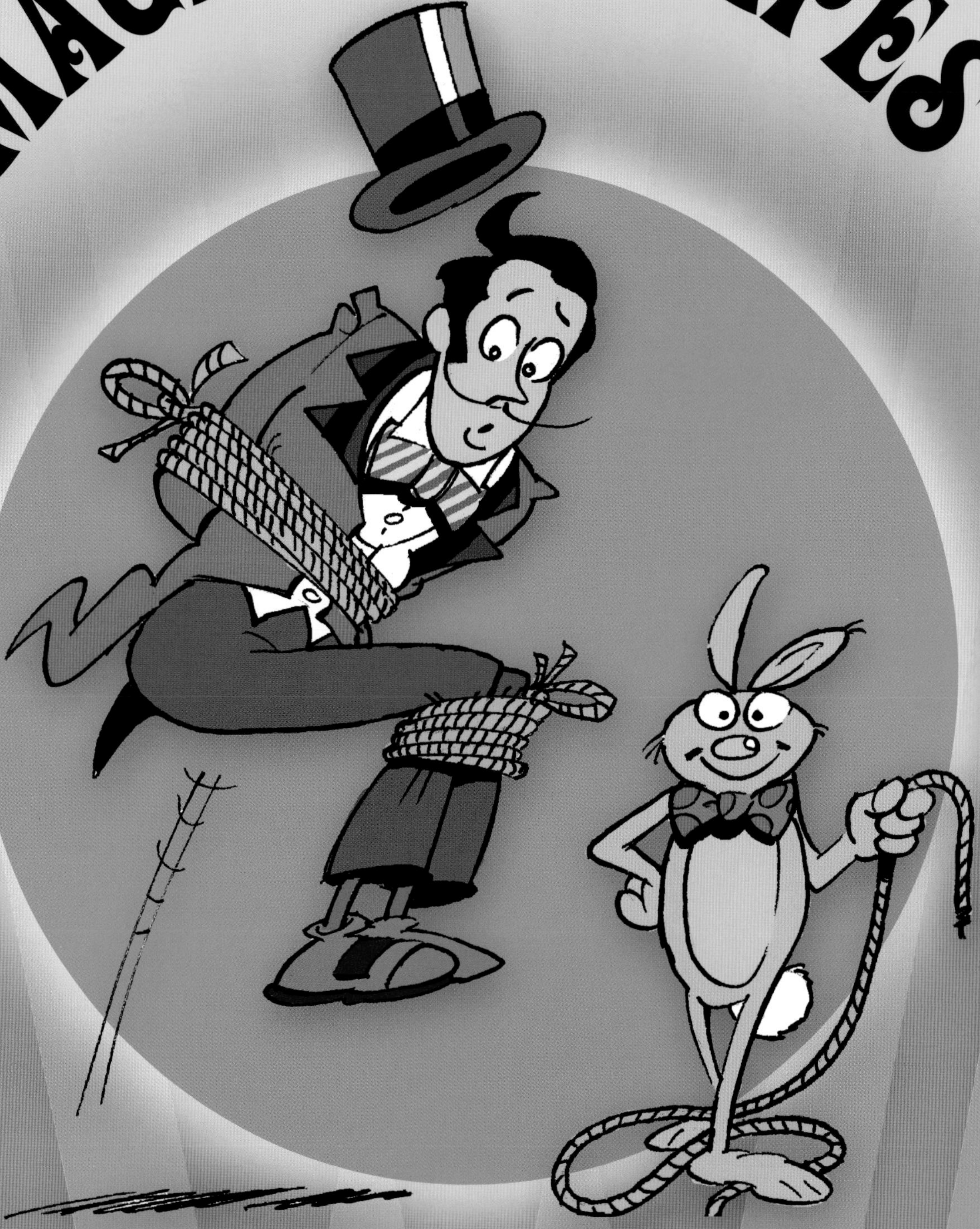

DISAPPEARING COIN

1 Prior to the trick, the magician makes a slit in the lining of his necktie near the bottom. It should be big enough to slip a coin in and out easily.

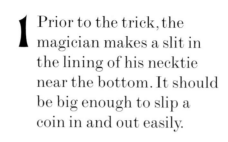

2 To perform the trick, the magician holds a coin in his right hand and the corner of a dark handkerchief in his left. Both his hands are level with his chest and his tie is hanging loose.

3 He moves his right hand behind the handkerchief. As he does so he slips the coin into the slit in his tie, then pinches the tie to keep the coin in place. This takes a little practice to do convincingly.

4 The magician is now holding the tip of his tie (with the coin inside it) behind the dangling handkerchief.

5 He raises his right hand so that the coin (which is still inside the tie) bulges up inside the handkerchief. He pinches that bulge with his left hand and lets his right hand fall away.

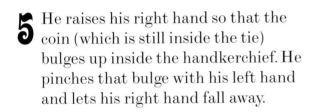

6 The magician calls for a volunteer to feel the coin by pinching the handkerchief.

DISAPPEARING COIN

7 The magician takes his left hand away. The volunteer is now holding the handkerchief (with the coin and tie pinched inside.)

8 The magician takes one corner of the handkerchief in each hand and asks the volunteer to let go. The magician holds up the handkerchief to the volunteer and spectators. The coin has disappeared!

MAGIC TIP!
WHY NOT WEAR A "FORMAL" OUTFIT FOR YOUR TRICKS – A JACKET, TIE, AND TOP HAT IF YOU CAN FIND ONE? THIS HELPS TO DISTRACT THE AUDIENCE FROM THE "BUSINESS" (TRICKERY) USED IN MAGIC ACTS.

THE RUNAWAY NUMBER

ILLUSION

A number seems to transfer from a dissolving sugar cube onto a volunteer's hand.

1 The magician asks for a volunteer to help him.

2 The magician asks the volunteer to pick a number from one to ten.

3 The volunteer calls out the number and the magician writes it on one side of a sugar cube. The magician must use a pencil, not a pen, to write the number.

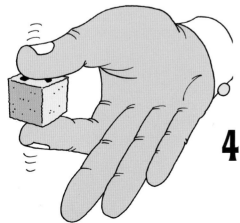

4 The magician takes the sugar cube and holds it tightly between his thumb and index finger. The side with the number should be touching his thumb.

5 The magician drops the sugar cube into a glass of cold water.

6 He takes the volunteer's hand, palm up, and holds it over the glass. The magician must be sure to press his thumb firmly against the volunteer's hand.

7 As the sugar cube dissolves, the magician says that the number has magically transferred onto the volunteer's hand. The magician releases the volunteer's hand. He asks the volunteer to show her palm to the audience. The number is clearly visible on it!

VANISHING MARBLE

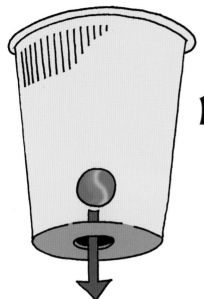

1 Prior to the trick, the magician cuts a hole in the bottom of a paper cup. The hole must be big enough for a marble to pass through.

ILLUSION
A marble dropped into a paper cup disappears – then reappears from inside the magician's pocket!

2 The magician puts a marble (identical to the one he'll be using in the trick) into his right-hand jacket pocket.

3 The magician begins the trick by holding the paper cup in his left hand. His hand forms a bowl beneath the cup.

VANISHING MARBLE

4 He holds a marble in his right hand and says he will make it disappear.

5 He drops the marble into the cup. It passes through the hole and lands in his left palm.

6 The magician tilts his left hand so that the marble rolls a little.

7 He grips the cup tightly so that the marble is pinched between the bottom of the cup and his palm.

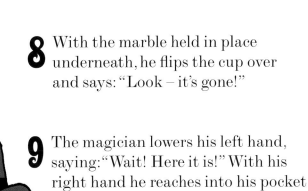

8 With the marble held in place underneath, he flips the cup over and says: "Look – it's gone!"

9 The magician lowers his left hand, saying: "Wait! Here it is!" With his right hand he reaches into his pocket and pulls out the spare marble.

10 He passes the marble round for the spectators to check, and puts the cup and the other marble out of sight.

ESCAPING COIN

1 The magician holds a coin by the edges between the thumb and third finger of his left hand.

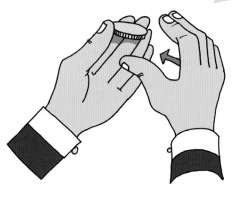

2 He pretends to grab the coin by moving his right hand up to it.

3 His right thumb passes under the coin and his fingers pass above it. The coin is covered by his right hand.

4 The magician makes a fist with his right hand and pulls it away. But he simply pulls away an empty fist. He allows the coin to drop into his left palm. He lets his left hand "go dead" by dropping it down with its back to the audience. The spectators think the coin is in his right hand.

5 The magician opens his right hand. There's nothing there! Then he straightens the fingers of his left hand to reveal the coin back there again.

WHO'S WATCHING THE WATCH?

1 Prior to the trick, the magician secretly chooses a partner who will be in on the trick.

ILLUSION

A volunteer's wristwatch disappears from beneath the magician's handkerchief.

2 The partner sits in the audience.

3 The magician begins the trick by asking to borrow a spectator's watch.

WHO'S WATCHING THE WATCH?

4 The magician takes the watch in his right hand. He flips his hand over and covers it with a dark handkerchief.

5 The magician gets the spectators to come up and feel the watch under the handkerchief. (The partner waits for the others to go, then goes up last.)

6 As the partner approaches, the magician waves his left hand slowly to distract the spectators. He widens his eyes and says, "This trick fooled even the great Houdini!" While the magician is saying this, the partner grasps the wristwatch and hides it in his clenched fist. He walks back to his seat.

7 The magician whisks the handkerchief away. He opens his hand – the watch has disappeared!

GOOFY GRAPES

1 The magician performs this trick while seated behind a table. He has hidden one grape in his lap and set three others on the table.

ILLUSION

The magician makes several grapes disappear – and reappear just as quickly!

2 He begins by saying "I'm going to get rid of one grape." He picks up a grape with his left hand and drops his hand behind the table. Spectators think he's dropped the grape.

3 But he has held onto the grape and picked up the hidden grape. He hides the two grapes in three curved fingers as he brings his hand back up.

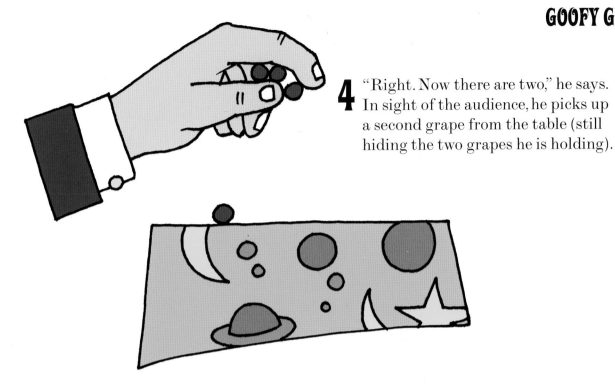

4 "Right. Now there are two," he says. In sight of the audience, he picks up a second grape from the table (still hiding the two grapes he is holding).

5 The magician puts all three grapes (the hidden two plus the one he has just picked up) into his right hand beneath the table. He does this quickly and closes his hand. The audience thinks he has one grape in his left hand, thrown one away and still has one on the table.

6 "OK," he says, "let's get rid of the last one." This time he really does push the remaining grape into his lap.

7 He finishes by saying: "So that leaves one, two, three grapes on the table." He counts the hidden grapes out from his right hand.

ELASTIC BAND JUMP

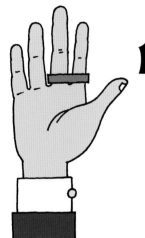

1 The magician places an elastic band over the index and middle fingers of his right hand. The back of his hand is facing the audience. He pulls the band down to the base of his fingers.

2 Now the magician walks among the spectators, asking them to pull on the band to make sure it's real.

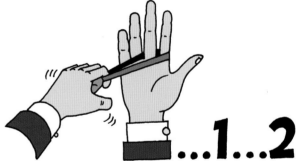

...1...2

3 The magician holds his right hand up again, as he did at the start of the trick. He says that on the count of three he will make the band jump along his hand to the last two fingers. He pulls back the band, releases it and says "One." He does the same on the count of "Two."

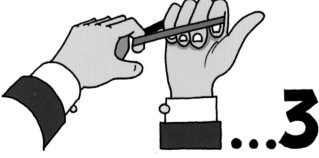

...3

4 As he pulls the band back for the third time, he curls all four fingers inside it.

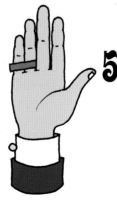

5 When the magician releases the band on "Three!" it jumps to his last two fingers.

67

TOOTHPICK TRICKERY

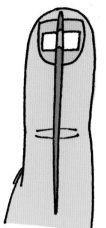

1 Prior to the trick, the magician uses a piece of clear tape to stick a toothpick to his right thumbnail. The toothpick should not jut out over the top of the thumb.

ILLUSION
With a single wave, the magician can make a toothpick disappear – and reappear.

2 The magician gets the toothpick in position by covering his thumbnail with his index finger and bending his thumb. With enough bending, the toothpick will stand up nearly straight. To perform the trick, the magician says he can make the toothpick disappear with a single wave of his hand.

3 He asks the spectators to watch closely as he does the trick. The magician swipes his left hand in front of his right hand. As it passes, he straightens his thumb, so that the toothpick is concealed.

4 The magician holds up his hands to the audience, who can't see the toothpick because it is nestled behind his thumb.

MAGIC TIP
THE MAGICIAN BENDS HIS RIGHT THUMB AGAIN TO MAKE THE TOOTHPICK REAPPEAR.

THIMBLE MYSTERY

ILLUSION

The magician magically makes a thimble disappear.

1 Prior to the trick, the magician makes sure the side pockets of his jacket are open so that he can drop things into them quickly. To perform the trick, the magician tells his spectators that he will use an ordinary pencil as a wand to help him make something disappear. He will start with something small – like a thimble. He holds the pencil in his right hand and the thimble in his left. He closes his fist over the thimble.

ONE...

TWO...

2 He reminds the spectators that it takes three taps of the wand to make the trick work. He raises the pencil until it is just behind his right ear. Then, on the count of "ONE," he swings the pencil down and taps his closed left hand.

3 The magician then raises the pencil to his right ear again. On the count of "TWO," he swings it down and taps his left hand again.

69

THIMBLE MYSTERY

...THREE!

4 He raises the pencil once more, but this time rests it behind his right ear. On the count of "THREE," he extends his index finger and swings it down (just as he did with the pencil). He holds up his right hand and says, "Whoops – I've made the wrong thing disappear!"

IT'S BEHIND YOUR EAR!!!

5 The magician continues to look at his right hand. When someone shouts: "It's behind your ear," he flutters his right hand and goes to grab the pencil.

6 He makes a fuss about yanking the pencil from behind his ear, saying: "I hope it's not stuck!" He even twists his body a little to give the spectators a better view of his fumbling. As he distracts the spectators in this way, he secretly moves his left hand back and lets the thimble drop into his jacket pocket. He keeps his left hand clenched and raises it again.

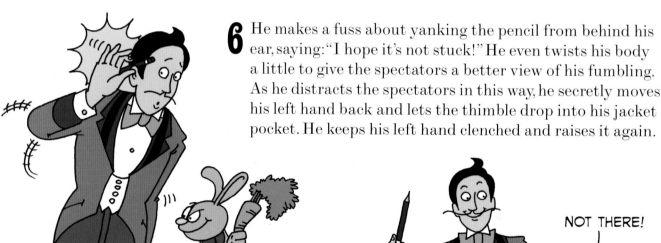

NOT THERE!

7 The magician finishes by saying he still thought the trick worked. He opens his left hand – and there's no thimble!

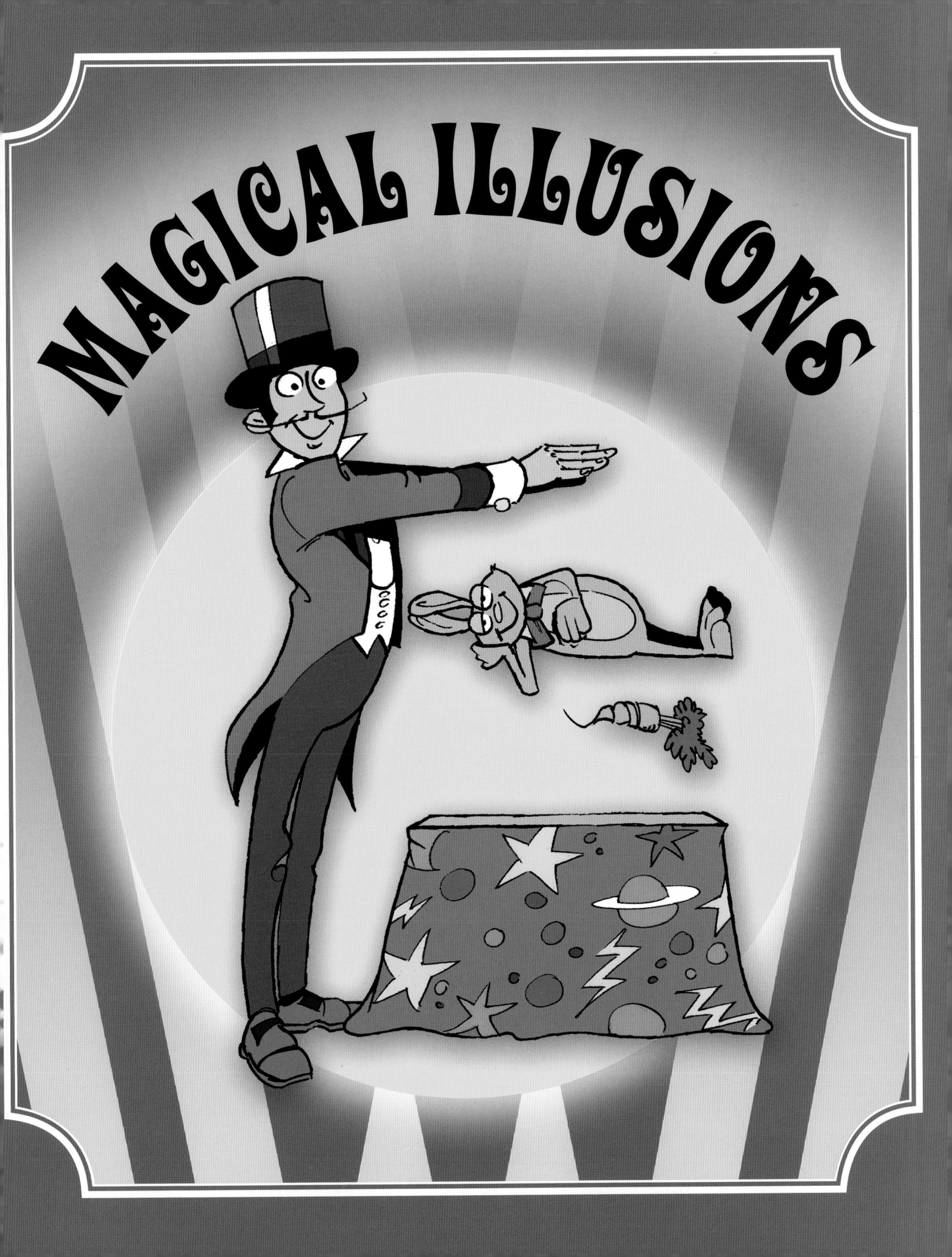
MAGICAL ILLUSIONS

SPOON BEND

1 The magician picks up a spoon and cups it between his hands.

2 He holds the spoon so that his interlocking fingers hide the handle. The bowl of the spoon should jut out between his left and right little fingers.

3 He says that he will bend the spoon using his magical powers. He presses the bowl of the spoon against the table.

4 The magician pulls a face to make it look as though he is concentrating hard. He begins to loosen the grip of his fingers.

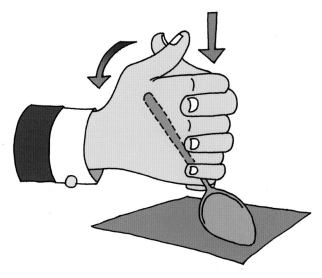

5 The bowl of the spoon moves forward. At the same time (and hidden from the spectators), the spoon handle swings across the palms of the magician's cupped hands. This sleight of hand makes it look as though the spoon has bent.

6 The magician quickly unlocks his fingers, picks up the spoon and shows it to the spectators to prove that it's back to normal.

PING-PONG PALM

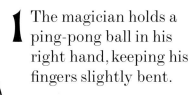

1 The magician holds a ping-pong ball in his right hand, keeping his fingers slightly bent.

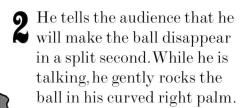

2 He tells the audience that he will make the ball disappear in a split second. While he is talking, he gently rocks the ball in his curved right palm.

3 As the magician rocks his hand, he raises his little finger slightly. The ball rolls against his little finger and stops.

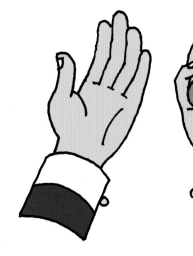

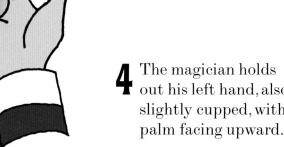

4 The magician holds out his left hand, also slightly cupped, with the palm facing upward.

5 While the audience is distracted by the left hand, the magician curls his third and fourth right fingers over a little more. The ball now rests between these two fingers.

6 In one motion, the magician tightens his third and fourth fingers (holding the ball in place) and flips his right hand so that the palm is facing downward.

7 He passes his right hand over his cupped left hand. It looks as though the ball is dropping into his left hand.

8 The magician closes his left hand before his right hand has passed completely over it.

NOT THERE

9 He moves his right hand down to his side and concentrates on holding his cupped left hand out. Then he slowly opens it to reveal – no ball!

THE PLASTIC WAND

ILLUSION

The magician uses a magic hair from a member of the audience to guide a plastic wand back and forth.

1 Prior to the trick, the magician slices the end off a ziplock sandwich bag. He leaves about as much plastic below the zip as there is above it.

2 He snips a small strip off one end of this piece of plastic. The bit he snips should be narrower than his little finger.

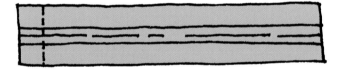

3 He secretly asks one of the spectators to be in on the trick later on.

76

4 The magician begins the trick by holding the plastic strip near the end he has snipped. His thumb is behind the strip and his index finger is in front of it.

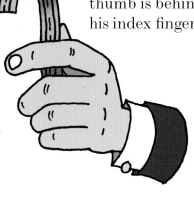

5 He tells the spectators that this is his plastic wand, even though it is flopping forward and looks nothing like a magician's wand.

6 The magician asks the spectators whether anyone has magic hair. He looks around and chooses his partner from the audience.

7 The magician's partner comes up and stands next to him. (The magician is still holding the wand in his hand.) The magician says, "Ah yes, definitely magic hair …" and pretends to pluck a hair from his partner's head.

THE PLASTIC WAND

8 The magician holds the "hair" over the end of the wand. He pretends to wrap it round the wand a few times.

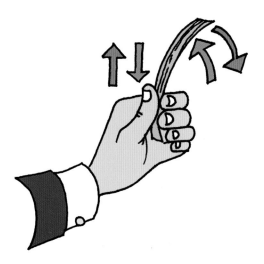

9 As he does this, he slowly drags his thumb along the wand. The end of the wand seems to be pulled back by the magic hair. The magician waves his other hand (with the magic hair) over the wand. He moves his thumb up the wand so that it seems to be pulled forward by the hair.

10 Finally, the magician pulls the magic hair (and wand) back and "drops" the magic hair. He slides his thumb quickly up the wand so that it flops forward.

DISAPPEARING STRAW

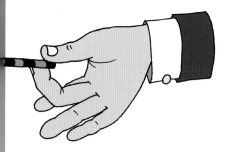

1 The magician holds a short length of drinking straw (about as long as his little finger) in his right hand, between the tip of his thumb and the tip of his middle finger. A little bit of the straw extends below his finger.

ILLUSION

The magician taps a piece of drinking straw into his right hand. But when he opens his hand, the straw has disappeared!

2 He makes sure that the straw is pointing straight up and his right palm is facing away from the audience. He announces that he will make the straw disappear.

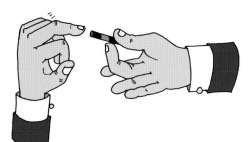

3 He starts to tap the straw down with the tip of his left middle finger. He keeps the fingers of his left hand together and slightly bent as he taps.

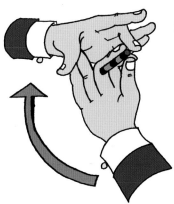

4 When the straw is almost tapped down, the magician taps the straw forward a little. The straw swings and the end of it hits the magician's left palm.

5 The magician secretly presses the straw into his left hand. (His left "tapping finger" presses it harder into his palm.) At the same time he clenches his right fist to make it look as though he's holding the straw there.

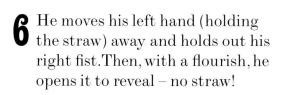

6 He moves his left hand (holding the straw) away and holds out his right fist. Then, with a flourish, he opens it to reveal – no straw!

THE RESTORED NAPKIN

1 The magician needs two paper napkins to make this trick work. He scrunches one of them into a tight ball and keeps it hidden in his slightly closed right hand.

ILLUSION

The magician tears up a paper napkin, but at the end of the trick the napkin is revealed in one piece!

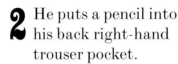

2 He puts a pencil into his back right-hand trouser pocket.

3 To start the trick, the magician tells the spectators he is going to tear a napkin and then restore it with his wand. He holds up a paper napkin and unfolds it. (He is still holding the scrunched-up napkin in his right hand.) He holds the napkin, stretched open, by the corners.

4 The magician tears the open napkin in half. He puts the pieces on top of each other and tears again. Now he has four pieces. The magician shows the spectators the pieces and then does another tear – now he has eight pieces.

5 He scrunches all of these pieces into a tight little ball (like the hidden ball) and closes his right hand over it. The other ball is sitting next to it, still hidden.

6 The magician says, "Now it's time to do some magic. Where's my wand?" In sight of the audience, he passes the un-torn napkin ball from his closed right hand and holds it up with his left hand. He waves this ball in his left hand to distract the spectators. The ball made of torn pieces is still hidden in his right hand.

THE RESTORED NAPKIN

7 With his right hand, he quickly stuffs the torn-up napkin ball into his back pocket and pulls out the pencil. He waves the pencil-wand over his left hand several times, then puts the wand down.

8 He slowly begins to unravel the ball in his left hand to reveal – a complete napkin!

FLOATING WATER

1 The magician shows the spectators a normal juice glass (made of glass, not plastic). He fills it to the brim with water.

ILLUSION
With just a few magic words, the magician manages to get a piece of card to hold back a whole glassful of water.

2 He shows the audience a piece of thin card. He says he will give the card the magical power to hold the water in the glass – even when it's upside down.

3 He holds the glass in one hand and the card in the other and turns his back to the spectators.

FLOATING WATER

4 The magician places the card on the rim of the glass, making sure it covers the glass completely. He continues to hold the glass with one hand and presses the card down on the rim.

5 Next the magician turns to the spectators again. He turns the glass upside down while holding the card tight against the rim.

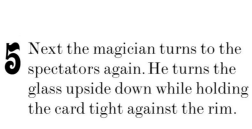

6 The magician speaks to the card: "Now it's time to do your magic. Keep that water inside the glass." He takes his hand away and the card stays in place – no water comes out of the glass!

SAW THE LADY IN HALF

1 Prior to the trick, the magician gets an empty envelope (from a medium-sized birthday card) and a blank piece of A4 paper. The envelope must be narrower than the A4 paper.

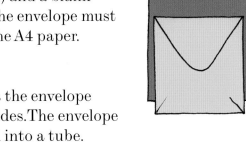

2 The magician seals the envelope and snips off the sides. The envelope can now be opened into a tube.

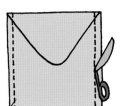

3 The magician cuts two slits across the back of the envelope, about a third of the way from each end.

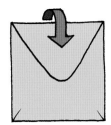

4 He cuts a vertical strip from the length of A4 paper. The strip should be a little narrower than the slits on the envelope.

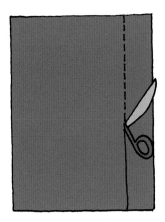

5 The magician draws a picture of a lady on this strip. She can be just a stick figure, but she should extend the whole length of the strip, with her head near one end and her feet at the other.

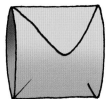
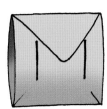

SAW THE LADY IN HALF

6 The magician makes sure the lady can slide through both of the slits.

7 To perform the classic "saw the lady in half" trick, the magician holds up the lady and the "box" into which she'll be placed. He makes sure the audience can't see the side with the slits.

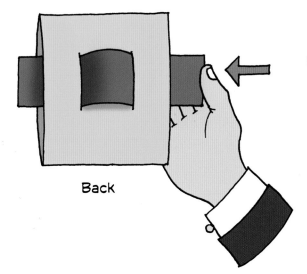

Back

8 He begins to slide the lady slowly into the box. But the audience can't see that he is sliding her out of the back of the envelope through the first slit and back in through the second slit.

9 With the lady sticking out of each end of the box, the magician lays the envelope flat on the table. He slowly cuts it in half. He makes sure that the scissors don't cut through the lady, but pass over the top of her.

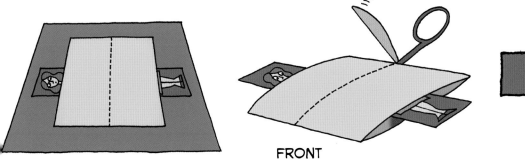

FRONT

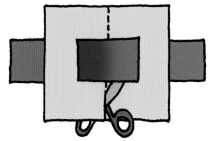

10 The magician slowly pulls the lady back through the envelope and holds her up to show that she has not been cut in half.

11 He finishes by holding up the two halves of the cut envelope, then crumpling them up and throwing them away before anyone can see the slits.

WHERE'S THE ORANGE?

ILLUSION

The magician shows a paper carrier bag to the spectators, then fills it with coins, a pen, a notebook and an orange. He decides to eat the orange – but it has turned into a lemon!

1 Prior to the trick, the magician finds a paper carrier bag. He makes sure that the spectators will be no closer than several paces when he does the trick.

2 He cuts a large orange in two and carefully scoops out the flesh.

3 He puts a lemon inside one orange half and carefully reassembles the orange.

4 He places the hollowed-out orange in a bowl containing a couple of other oranges. He should try to avoid revealing the seam where the orange was cut.

5 To perform the trick, the magician sits behind a table with the folded bag, a pencil, a pen, a small notebook and the bowl of oranges in front of him.

6 He opens the bag and shows it to the spectators. It's important that the spectators see the bag is empty. To make sure they look inside, the magician says, "This sort of flat-bottomed bag holds my stuff really well."

7 He places the bag upright on the table. Then he puts the things in the bag, saying, "Right, I'll need a pencil, maybe a pen, and this notebook."

WHERE'S THE ORANGE?

8 The magician says:"I might get hungry. I'll take an orange." He puts the hollowed-out orange from the fruit bowl into the bag. Then he says,"Mmm ...that orange looked tasty. Maybe I'll have it now."

9 He reaches inside the bag, flips the orange open and pulls out the lemon.

10 He holds up the lemon and says, "Wait a minute – wasn't that an orange a few seconds ago?!"

ELASTIC BAND UP THE NOSE

1 Prior to the trick, the magician arranges some props – pieces of fruit, a tennis ball, some string, even things he won't be using – on the table.

ILLUSION

The magician paces round a table full of props, secretly fingering an elastic band. He absent-mindedly holds the band near his nose and gives a sniff. The band seems to disappear up his nostril!

2 He loops an elastic band round his right wrist.

3 While walking slowly round the table, the magician stops now and then to pick up some of the props. As he holds a prop, he says "I wonder what that's for," or "That looks interesting." Then he puts it down and continues.

91

ELASTIC BAND UP THE NOSE

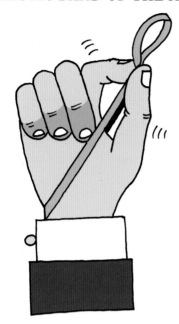

4 As he continues to walk round the table he chooses a moment when his back is to the audience, then he pulls on the elastic band with his left hand and pinches it between his right thumb and index finger.

5 The magician is now holding an elastic loop about half as long as his little finger.

6 He faces the spectators again. He holds the loop up and says, "What's this? An elastic band. Hmm. Don't need that right now."

7 With a quick motion he puts the band up to his nose and lets go. He makes a loud sniff as he does this, so that the audience won't hear the band snapping back.

8 The spectators think he has sniffed the elastic band into his nostril!

BRAIN GAMES

MIND-READING

1 Prior to the trick, the magician chooses an assistant who will be in on it. The magician tells the assistant the trick depends on him clenching and unclenching his teeth, so that his face muscles tighten and relax. The magician rehearses placing his hands on the assistant's temples – the soft bits at the side of the forehead.

2 To perform the trick, the magician asks for a volunteer from the audience to help him with a mind-reading trick. He picks the secret assistant.

3 The magician says he will leave the room. Before he goes, he asks the other spectators to write down a four-digit number, show it to the assistant, and then hide the paper.

4 The magician leaves the room while the spectators do this, then he returns to face the assistant.

5 The magician looks the assistant in the eye, then raises his hands to the assistant's face so that they cover his cheeks. The magician's middle fingertips should lightly touch each temple.

6 The magician says he will read the assistant's mind to learn the secret number. The assistant clenches his teeth and the magician counts the number of clenches. In this way, the assistant signals the four digits that were written on the paper. He pauses after each set of clenches. So, for the number 5478 he clenches five times, then four, then seven, then eight.

7 Slowly the magician takes his hands away from the assistant's head. He closes his eyes as if imagining the number, then speaks it out loud to the stunned audience!

MATCHING ANSWERS

1 The magician places ten small pieces of paper, two pencils, and two mugs on a table. Then he asks for a volunteer from the audience.

2 He gives the volunteer five pieces of paper, a pencil, and a mug. The magician keeps the rest for himself.

3 The magician says he will ask the volunteer five simple questions. He tells the volunteer to write each of her answers, with its number, on a slip of paper. Then he asks her to fold the paper and place it in the mug. The magician says he will write his predictions on his five pieces of paper. He will try to match the volunteer's answers.

4 Each question is simple enough to have a one-word answer. The first could be "What city would you like to visit?"

MATCHING ANSWERS

5 The volunteer writes down her answer and puts the paper into the mug. The magician writes "summer" on a piece of paper and puts it into his mug.

6 When both papers are in the mugs, the magician asks the volunteer what her first answer was. Let's imagine that the volunteer says "Rome."

7 Now the magician asks his second question, which could be: "What flower do you like best?" The volunteer writes down her answer and puts the paper into the mug. The magician writes "Rome" on a piece of paper and puts it into his mug.

8 The trick continues like this. Each time, the magician writes down the volunteer's answer to the previous question.

9 The magician's final question is: "Which season do you like best?". As the volunteer writes down her answer, which is most likely to be "summer," the magician writes down the volunteer's fourth answer. The magician asks another volunteer to read out both sets of answers. They match!

ROME

COIN DETECTOR

1 Prior to the trick, the magician makes sure his magic table is covered with a cloth with lots of curls and squiggles in the design. (This helps to disguise the secret hair.)

ILLUSION

At first guess, the magician finds a coin hidden under one of three bottle tops.

2 Next the magician plucks out one of his hairs and sticks it onto one side of a coin with a piece of clear tape. He trims the hair so that it extends beyond the edge of the coin by about half the coin's width. He puts the coin in his pocket.

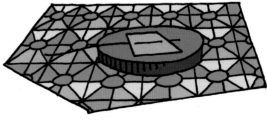

3 To perform the trick, the magician casually reaches into his pocket and pulls out the coin he has prepared. He puts it on the table.

4 The magician tells the audience he can sense the presence of a coin even when it is hidden from view. He takes three plastic bottle tops (they should be opaque, not clear, and slightly wider than the coin). He places them next to the coin.

5 The magician covers the coin with one of the bottle tops and places the other two tops on either side. "Right," he says, "the coin is under this top." He uncovers the coin – and the spectators laugh or groan!

COIN DETECTOR

6 "But I can do more," says the magician. He asks the spectators to slide the tops around on the table and line them up again – in any order – while his back is turned.

7 When the spectators have finished, the magician turns round to face them. He examines the tops – staring, sniffing and even listening to them. What he's really doing is looking for the tiny bit of hair sticking out.

8 Once he's sure, the magician picks up the top and reveals the coin underneath. Ta-dah!

SHOW ME YOUR MIND!

ILLUSION

A volunteer is asked to write down a series of important years and other numbers. He is then told to add them together. The magician guesses the sum exactly.

1 The magician chooses a volunteer and gives him a piece of paper and a pencil.

2 The magician turns his back to the volunteer and asks him to write down the answers to four questions. Each answer should be written directly beneath the previous one.

3 First, the magician asks: "What year were you born?" Then he asks: "In which year did something important happen to you?" The third question is: "How many years ago did that big event happen?" And the final question is: "What will your age be this year?"

```
  2003
  2008
     5
    10
  ────
  4026
```

4 Now the magician asks the volunteer to add up the four numbers.

2013 × 2 = 4026

5 While the volunteer is doing this, the magician thinks of the current year and doubles that number in his head.

6 The magician turns and tells the audience the number he has just calculated. Then he asks the volunteer to show his "secret number." They're the same!

4026

X-RAY VISION

1 The magician places the following props on a table: a small piece of paper, a felt-tip pen, a small brown envelope, a slightly larger white envelope, and a piece of dark construction paper.

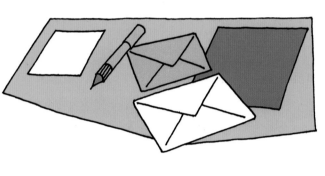

2 He asks for a volunteer to come up to the table. The magician stands behind the spectators, with his back to them.

3 He asks the volunteer to write a short word on the piece of paper, using the felt-tip pen.

4 The magician asks the volunteer to place the paper in the brown envelope and then to slip the brown envelope into the white envelope.

5 The magician asks the volunteer to hold up the white envelope so that the audience can see it. He asks the audience if they can read the word written inside. They can't.

6 The magician says: "It's now safe for me to turn round." He looks at the envelope. He can't read the word either.

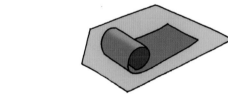

7 "I need to make an X-ray telescope," he says. He folds the construction paper in half and tears along the fold to make two strips.

8 The magician rolls up one strip to make a small tube. He holds it to his eye, like a telescope, and picks up the white envelope.

9 With the "X-ray telescope" touching the envelope, the magician can read the word hidden inside!

MAGIC TIP!
THE TUBE BLOCKS REFLECTED LIGHT FROM THE WHITE ENVELOPE, MAKING IT EASIER TO SEE THE WORD ON THE PAPER INSIDE.

THE COUNT OF SIX

1 Prior to the trick, the magician finds six small objects to use as props – sweets, crayons, paper clips, or anything he can hold easily.

2 He finds a blank card (about twice the size of a playing card) and a felt-tip pen.

3 To perform the trick, the magician stands behind a table with the six objects, card, and pen in front of him. He tells the audience that he will use these props to read a volunteer's mind.

TWO

4 He holds up the objects one by one, counting out one to six as he does so. He places the objects back down in no particular order – not in a straight line.

5 The magician asks a volunteer to come up and examine the objects. The volunteer chooses an object, but does not reveal which one it is.

6 The magician says he has read the volunteer's mind and knows the chosen object. He writes a number between 1 and 6 on the card and places it face down on the table.

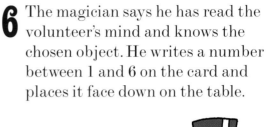

7 He rearranges the objects a little to distract the audience and asks the volunteer to point to his chosen object. The magician says, "Right, he has chosen object number X" (the number he has already written on the card.)

8 Then the magician says: "And the number I predicted was ..." and he flips over the card. It's the same number!

MAGIC TIP!
THIS TRICK RELIES ON THE POWER OF SUGGESTION. IT'S BEST TO USE SIX SIMILAR OBJECTS SO THE SPECTATORS ARE LESS LIKELY TO LINK EACH NUMBER TO A PARTICULAR ITEM.

AND THE YEAR IS...

1 Prior to the trick, the magician gathers together about ten or twelve coins. They should be of different value, but all from the same year. He puts them in his pocket.

2 To perform the trick, the magician asks for a volunteer from the audience. When the volunteer joins him, the magician turns his head away and reaches into his pocket for the coins. He makes it clear that he cannot see the coins in his hand. He asks the volunteer to pick one and look at it carefully.

3 The magician says he can tell by the coin's mysterious force what year it was made. The magician calls out the date and asks the volunteer to show the coin to the other spectators. It's the same year!

1993

1993

1993!!!

STOP THE PULSE!

ILLUSION

The magician says he has learnt the ancient trick of making his heart stop when he tells it to. Then he proves it to a volunteer!

1 Prior to the trick, the magician stuffs a pair of socks into his right armpit. He lowers his arm to keep the socks from falling down.

2 He invites a volunteer to join him. The magician tells the audience that he will stop his heart and that the volunteer will be his witness.

3 The magician holds out his right arm, taking care to keep the socks in place. He explains he is making it easier for the volunteer to take his pulse, on the inside of his wrist. He asks the volunteer to take his pulse. The volunteer puts her fingertips against the inside of the magician's wrist. When she finds the magician's pulse, she announces it to the audience.

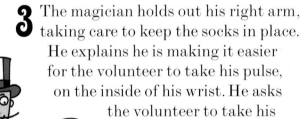

4 "Now," the magician says, "I will use my ancient powers to stop my heart. When I raise my left hand, the volunteer will test my pulse once more." The magician presses his right arm firmly against his body so the socks are tightly lodged. After about ten seconds, he raises his left hand. The volunteer puts her fingers to the magician's wrist. There's no pulse – no sign of a beating heart!

CRAZY CRAYONS

1 The magician places a box of eight crayons on the table. He asks the spectators to examine them to make sure they've not been marked or tampered with.

ILLUSION

Behind the magician's back, the spectators choose a crayon from a boxful. The magician is mysteriously able to pick it out from the rest.

2 The magician turns his back to the table, folding his hands behind him, and asks a spectator to pick a crayon and put it into his right hand.

3 Holding the crayon behind him, the magician turns to face the audience. With the crayon now hidden from view, he scrapes off a tiny bit of wax with his thumbnail.

4 The magician turns away again so the spectator can take the crayon and put it back in the box. The magician folds his hands in front of him and turns round. He puts his hands up to his head "to help concentrate." As he does so, he secretly notes the shade of the crayon wax under his thumbnail.

5 Now he examines the crayon box. He opens it slowly, decides which crayon matches the thumbnail wax, and pulls it out of the box.

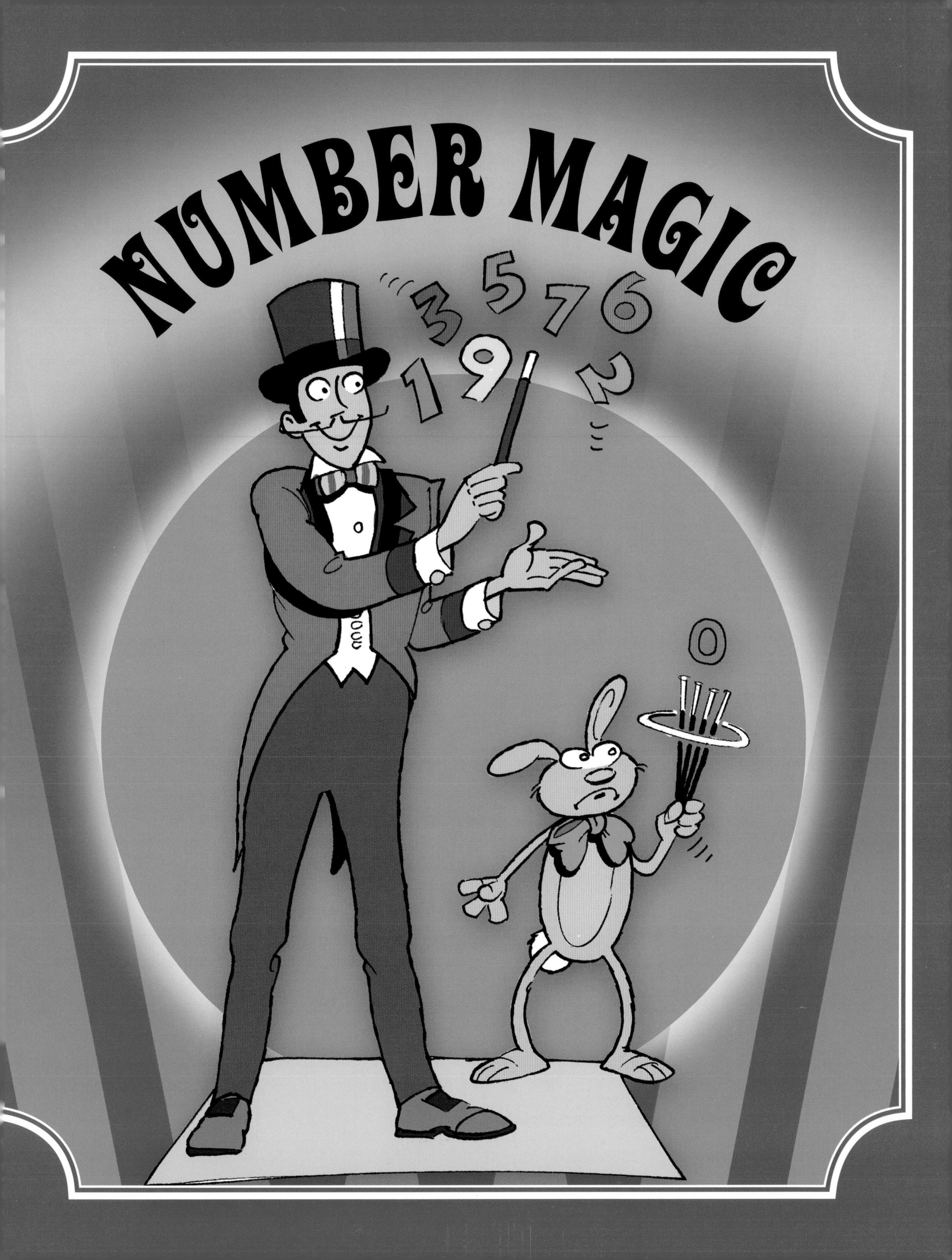
NUMBER MAGIC
3 5 7 6
1 9 2
0

CALENDAR ADDITION

1 The magician holds up a calendar, the sort that has a month on each page, and asks for a volunteer to join him.

ILLUSION

The magician appears to add together a random collection of nine numbers, picked from a calendar, in a split second.

2 The magician gives the volunteer the calendar and a felt-tip marker.

March

			1	2	3	4	5
6	7	8	9	10	11	12
13	14	15	16	17	18	19
20	21	22	23	24	25	26
27	28	29	30	31		

3 The magician says he's going to do some instant calculations, but it will involve writing on the calendar. So he asks the volunteer to turn the calendar to an early month in the year.

4 Now he asks the volunteer to draw round a group of nine numbers on that page. They can be any nine numbers, but they must form a square three numbers wide and three numbers deep.

112

```
10
11
12
17
18
19
24
25
26 +
─────
162
```

5 The magician asks the volunteer and the spectators to add up the nine numbers.

162

MAGIC TIP!
THE MAGICIAN GETS HIS ANSWER BY MULTIPLYING THE MIDDLE NUMBER OF THE SQUARE BY NINE. IT'S ALWAYS RIGHT!

6 As they all start adding in their heads or on paper, the magician butts in, saying: "I've got it! The answer is XXX."

GIVE ME FIVE!

1 The magician asks the spectators to put their thinking caps on because they're going to be going on a mental workout.

ILLUSION

The magician gets the spectators to work on their own secret number in different ways. At the end of the calculations, he predicts the correct answer – for everyone!

2 He says: "But I'll know your answer before you have a chance to work it out. First step – pick a number and keep it secret."

3 The magician tells the spectators that the number they choose can be large or small. But he warns them that they'll be doing some multiplication, addition, division, and subtraction with it – so they need to bear this in mind when choosing.

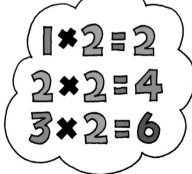

$$1 \times 2 = 2$$
$$2 \times 2 = 4$$
$$3 \times 2 = 6$$

4 The magician asks the spectators to double their number.

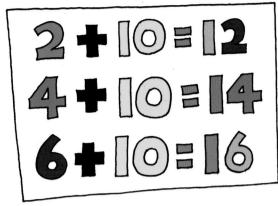

5 He asks them to add 10 to the new number.

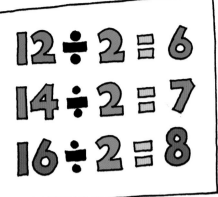

6 He asks them to divide that number by two.

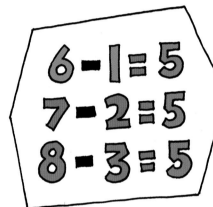

7 Finally he asks the spectators to subtract their original number from the one in Step 6.

MAGIC TIP!
THIS ANSWER WORKS FOR EVERY NUMBER, BUT THE MAGICIAN DOESN'T TELL ANYONE HIS SECRET!

8 The magician asks the spectators to line up and approach him one by one. He tells them to keep their final number to themselves. When each spectator reaches the magician, he whispers that the answer is "5."

NUMBERS ON THE BRAIN

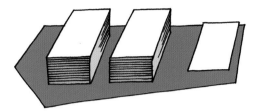

1 Prior to the trick, the magician obtains 21 blank index cards. He divides 20 of them into two piles of ten cards. He marks the first set of cards 1 to 10 in big numbers.

ILLUSION

The magician gets a volunteer to do some tricky calculations and then guesses the secret number the volunteer ends up with.

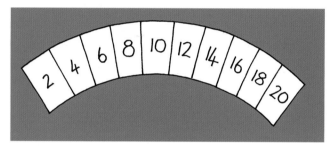

2 He marks the second set 2, 4, 6, 8, 10, 12, 14, 16, 18, 20.

3 He places the first set of cards face down on the table. He spreads the second set face up so that the numbers on the cards are visible. He leaves the spare blank card on the table, next to a pencil.

4 The magician asks for a volunteer to pick a card from the first set. (Let's say that 2 is picked.) The volunteer looks at the card and shows it to the other spectators, but not the magician. Then he puts it face down on its own on the table.

5 The magician asks the volunteer to double the number he has picked (in this case, it will be 4.)

6 The magician asks the volunteer to pick a card from the second set and show it to everyone (including the magician.) This card is important, so the magician makes sure he remembers it. Let's say that 12 is picked.

7 The magician asks the volunteer to add this number to the one he has in his head. (The other spectators will probably be doing this too.) The sum of the two numbers in our example is 16.

8 Now the magician asks the volunteer to divide the new number by two, and then to subtract the original, secret number from that. The result in our example is 6.

$$16 \div 2 = 8$$

$$8 - 2 = 6$$

117

NUMBERS ON THE BRAIN

9 The magician asks the volunteer to write this final number on the blank card on the table and to turn that card face down.

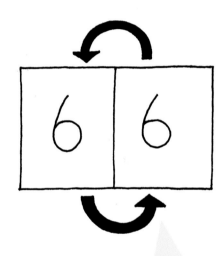

10 The magician goes over to the card and writes a number on the back of it. (This number will be half the number that the volunteer picked in step 6 – but the magician doesn't tell anyone this!)

11 The magician flips the card over. The numbers are the same on both sides!

MAGIC TIP!
THIS TRICK WORKS BEST IF YOU ASK FOR A VOLUNTEER WHO'S REALLY QUICK AT MENTAL ARITHMETIC. THIS WILL MAKE THE "MAGIC" SEEM EVEN MORE AMAZING!

ELEVEN FINGERS

1 The magician tells the spectators he can prove that he has eleven fingers. With his left index finger he counts the digits on his right hand, starting with the thumb –"one, two, three, four, five." Then, using his right index finger, he counts the fingers on his left hand –"six, seven, eight, nine, ten."

2 The magician looks a little puzzled as he stares at his fingers:"Ten? I thought it was eleven!"

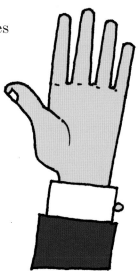

3 Using his right index finger, he counts back along his left-hand fingers – "ten, nine, eight, seven, six ..." Then he holds up his outstretched left hand and says: "...plus five makes eleven!"

SURPRISING SUM

ILLUSION

The magician asks a volunteer to do some calculations with a large secret number. But the magician arrives at the same answer as the volunteer – in an instant!

1 The magician asks a volunteer to choose a three-digit number, with all three digits the same (such as 222 or 777).

2 He turns away and asks the volunteer to whisper this number to the other spectators.

3 The magician asks the volunteer to add up the digits. (Of course, most of the other spectators will be doing the same thing, which will make the result even better.)

$$555 \div 15 = 37$$

4 The magician then asks the volunteer to divide the original number by the second number.

5 When it looks as though the volunteer has come up with an answer, the magician calls out "37!"

6 The spectators probably won't have figured it out, but the answer is always 37!

120

SEE-THROUGH DICE

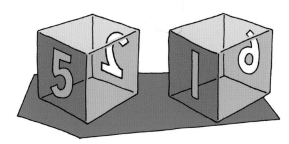

1 Prior to the trick, the magician examines a pair of dice to remind himself that opposite sides of the same dice always add up to seven. Therefore, if there's a six on one side, the opposite side will be a one, a five will be opposite a two, and so on.

2 The magician holds up the two dice and asks the spectators to examine them.

3 He chooses a volunteer to help him prove that there's no cheating involved in this trick. The magician hands the dice to the volunteer and turns his back to them.

SEE-THROUGH DICE

4 He tells the volunteer to roll the dice.

5 Once the dice are rolled, the magician turns round and waves his hands slowly over them. He tells the spectators he is picking up magic vibrations.

4 AND 2

6 He announces that he has picked up the vibrations and can predict what the hidden sides will be. He looks at the numbers on the faces of the dice and subtracts each one from seven. He announces the results as the "hidden numbers." The volunteer picks up the dice – to reveal the magician's predictions!

HUMAN CALCULATOR

1 The magician hands a volunteer a piece of paper, pencil and calculator.

ILLUSION

The magician races against a spectator to work out a sum. Although the spectator uses a calculator and the magician doesn't, the magician wins!

```
7  9  3
2  6  1
5  8  4
```

2 He asks the volunteer to write a three-digit number on the paper. Then he asks two other spectators to each write a three-digit number on the same sheet of paper.

```
7  9  3
2  6  1
5  8  4
2  0  6
7  3  8
```

3 The magician takes the paper, which now has a column of three numbers. He says, "I can add these up in my head." Then he says: "No – that's too easy – I'll add two more numbers!" He writes two more three-digit numbers underneath the three numbers. He takes a little time writing them because he needs to look closely at the first and second numbers in the column.

HUMAN CALCULATOR

4 The magician asks another volunteer to count down from ten. When the volunteer reaches zero, this is the signal for the first volunteer to start adding up the five numbers with the calculator. In a couple of seconds the magician calls out the right answer – before the volunteer has finished keying in the numbers!

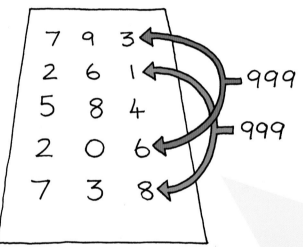

EXACTLY THE SAME NUMBER

ILLUSION

A volunteer is asked to write a number on a slip of paper. The magician gets a laugh – or a groan – by writing exactly the same number on a separate slip of paper.

1 The magician hands a volunteer a slip of paper and a pencil. He then asks the volunteer to go to the other side of the room.

2 The magician asks the volunteer to write a number – as big as he likes – on his slip of paper, then to fold the slip and hand it to another spectator ("the judge") for safe keeping.

3 The magician then says, "I am going to write exactly the same number on my slip of paper." He writes on his paper, folds it over, and hands it to the judge (who now has both slips.)

4 The magician asks the judge to read the first slip clearly. Then he asks her to read the second one (the magician's slip.) It reads: "Exactly the same number." The magician bows and says, "See – I told you I'd write exactly the same number!"

MISSING DOMINO

1 The magician displays a set of dominos, face up, on a table.

2 He asks a volunteer to flip the dominos over and shuffle them. He then asks the volunteer to name a number between four and ten.

3 The magician looks hard at the table and chooses that number of dominos from the set. He slides them along the table, still face down, to form a little group.

4 The magician asks the volunteer to slide three of those dominos to one side. Now it's the magician's turn to choose one domino from the group. He slides one aside.

5 The magician asks the volunteer to flip over all the dominos – except the one he has kept aside.

127

MISSING DOMINO

6 The magician asks the volunteer to arrange the dominos in a circle so that the last one is almost back to the first. The right-hand number of one domino must match the left-hand number of the next.

7 The volunteer can't complete the chain because the numbers of the first and last dominos don't match. The magician takes his domino, flips it over, and slots it in to complete the chain.

MAGIC FACT
THE CHOOSING OF NUMBERS EARLY ON IN THE TRICK WAS SIMPLY A DISTRACTION. EVERY SET OF DOMINOS IS MADE TO LINK BACK TO ITSELF, SO ANY DOMINO TAKEN OUT WILL COMPLETE THE CHAIN.